Thanksgiving

A Buddy Book
by
Julie Murray

Visit us at
www.abdopub.com

Printed in the United States.

Edited by: Christy DeVillier
Contributing Editors: Matt Ray, Michael P. Goecke
Graphic Design: Denise Esner
Image Research: Deborah Coldiron
Cover Photograph: Eyewire Inc.
Interior Photographs: Corbis, Library of Congress, North Wind Picture Archives, Photodisc

Library of Congress Cataloging-in-Publication Data

Murray, Julie, 1969-
  Thanksgiving/Julie Murray.
    p. cm. — (Holidays)
  Summary: An introduction to the history, as well as the past and present celebration customs, of the holiday known as Thanksgiving Day.
  Includes bibliographical references and index.
  ISBN 1-57765-956-2
    1. Thanksgiving Day—Juvenile literature. [1. Thanksgiving Day. 2. Holidays.] I. Title.

GT4975 .M87 2003
394.2649—dc21

2002074669

Table of Contents

What Is Thanksgiving?

Thanksgiving is a **holiday** for giving thanks. It is a time for people to be thankful for what they have. It is a day for family and friends to be together. For many people, Thanksgiving is also a day for prayer.

Families gather together on Thanksgiving Day.

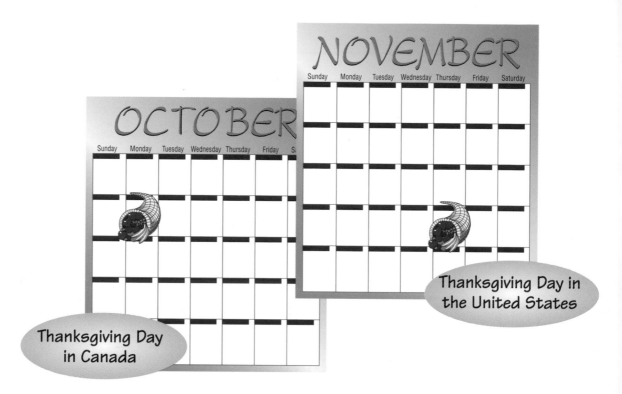

Thanksgiving Day in Canada

Thanksgiving Day in the United States

People in the United States and Canada celebrate Thanksgiving every year. Americans celebrate Thanksgiving on the fourth Thursday in November. In Canada, Thanksgiving Day is on the second Monday in October.

An Old Custom

Long ago, the Greeks and Romans held **harvest** festivals. They would celebrate and give thanks for a good harvest. A good harvest is when crops grow a lot of food. They celebrated with **feasts**, dancing, and parades. Maybe the idea of Thanksgiving began with these festivals.

People danced to celebrate a good harvest.

The Pilgrims' trip to America took 66 days.

The **Pilgrims** brought the Thanksgiving **custom** to America. The Pilgrims were from England, a country in Europe. They sailed to America on a boat called the *Mayflower*.

The Pilgrims arrived in America in 1620. They settled in Plymouth Rock, Massachusetts. Back then, America was a great **wilderness**.

The First Thanksgiving

The **Pilgrims'** first winter in America was hard. They did not have enough food. Many people died.

Winter was a tough time for the Pilgrims.

In the spring of 1621, the **Pilgrims** met the Wampanoag People. These Native Americans helped the Pilgrims. They shared what they knew about fishing, hunting, and farming. They gave the Pilgrims corn, beans, and squash to plant.

The Native Americans helped the Pilgrims.

The Native Americans knew which crops grow best in America.

The **Pilgrims** carefully tended their crops. Their crops grew a lot of food. The Pilgrims were happy to have a good **harvest**. This meant that they would not run out of food during the winter.

The Pilgrims thanked the Native Americans and invited them to a feast.

The **Pilgrims** decided to celebrate their good **harvest**. They invited the Wampanoag People to a **feast**. The Native Americans brought five deer. There may have been duck, seafood, fruits, and nuts to eat, too. People played games and told stories. This celebration is what many people call the First Thanksgiving. It lasted for three days.

Becoming A National Tradition

The Thanksgiving **custom** spread throughout America's 13 **colonies**. In 1777, all the Americans celebrated Thanksgiving on the same day. This was the first national Thanksgiving. They gave thanks for winning the Battle of Saratoga. This was a famous battle in the **American Revolution**.

The British lost to the Americans in the Battle of Saratoga.

Americans had a lot to be thankful for in 1789. This was the year they won their freedom from England. President George Washington made November 26, 1789, a national day of Thanksgiving. This was called the Thanksgiving **Proclamation**.

After 1789, many years went by without a national Thanksgiving. Many states celebrated the **holiday** at different times.

George Washington was the first president of the United States.

Sarah Josepha Hale

Sarah Josepha Hale was a writer in the 1800s. She wrote poems and children's stories. Hale also wrote for women's magazines.

Sarah Josepha Hale wrote the words to "Mary Had a Little Lamb."

Hale wrote about Thanksgiving in *Ladies' Magazine* and *Godey's Lady's Book*. She believed that Thanksgiving was an important **custom**. Hale thought Thanksgiving should be a national **holiday**. So, she began writing to United States presidents and statesmen. She wrote more than 1,000 letters.

Thanks to Hale, President Abraham Lincoln made Thanksgiving a national holiday. This happened in 1863. Lincoln set aside the last Thursday in November as Thanksgiving Day.

Make a Thanksgiving Basket

Ask an adult to help you gather:

- Old newspaper
- One medium-sized basket
- Pinecones, twigs, colorful leaves, acorns, or nuts
- Glue
- Gold and orange glitter
- Apples, small pumpkins, or dried corn

1. Cover your work area with the old newspapers.

2. Set aside: pinecones, a few acorns and nuts, and three eight-inch (20-cm) twigs. Break other twigs into smaller pieces. Put the smaller twigs and most of the acorns and nuts into the basket. Lay a few leaves on top.

3. Pour the glitter into two bowls, one for each color.

4. Carefully place small drops of glue on a pinecone. Sprinkle gold or orange glitter on the pinecone. Then, set aside.

5. Glue and glitter the other pinecones and items that were set aside. It may take 30 minutes for the glue to dry.

6. Place the apples, pumpkins, or dried corn in the basket. Add the glittered items when the glue has dried.

7. Place your Thanksgiving basket in a place for everyone to see!

America's Thanksgiving Today

Today, Thanksgiving is a national **holiday** in the United States. Schools and many businesses are closed on Thanksgiving Day.

On Thanksgiving Day, families and friends often get together for a **feast**. Turkey is often part of the Thanksgiving feast. Other Thanksgiving foods are sweet potatoes, stuffing, cranberry sauce, and pumpkin pie.

A turkey feast is common on Thanksgiving Day.

Giving thanks is an important part of celebrating Thanksgiving.

Some families pray together on Thanksgiving Day. Some people enjoy watching football games or parades on television. Others spend the **holiday** serving food to homeless people. Indeed, there are many ways to celebrate the Thanksgiving holiday.

Important Words

American Revolution the war Americans fought to win their freedom from England.

colony a settlement. Colonists are the people who live in a colony.

custom a practice that has been around a long time. Eating turkey is a Thanksgiving custom for Americans.

feast a large meal.

harvest what is gathered from ripe crops. A harvest may be vegetables, fruits, or grains.

holiday a special time for celebration.

Pilgrims the people who sailed from England in 1620 and settled in Plymouth Rock, Massachusetts.

proclamation a public announcement.

wilderness wild, unsettled land.

Web Sites

To learn more about Thanksgiving,

visit ABDO Publishing Company on the World Wide Web. Web site links about Thanksgiving are featured on our Book Links page. These links are routinely monitored and updated to provide the most current information available.

www.abdopub.com

Index